VETERINARIAN'S
TOOLS

MARY ELIZABETH SALZMANN

Consulting Editor, Diane Craig, M.A./Reading Specialist

A Division of ABDO

ABDO
Publishing Company

visit us at www.abdopublishing.com

Published by ABDO Publishing Company, a division of ABDO,
P.O. Box 398166, Minneapolis, Minnesota 55439. Copyright © 2011
by Abdo Consulting Group, Inc. International copyrights reserved in
all countries. No part of this book may be reproduced in any form
without written permission from the publisher. Super SandCastle™
is a trademark and logo of ABDO Publishing Company.

Printed in the United States of America,
North Mankato, Minnesota
092010
012011

 PRINTED ON RECYCLED PAPER

Editor: Katherine Hengel
Content Developer: Nancy Tuminelly
Photo Credits: Shutterstock
With special thanks to Minnehaha Animal Hospital,
Minneapolis, Minn. (www.minnehaahaanimalhospital.com)

Library of Congress Cataloging-in-Publication Data

Salzmann, Mary Elizabeth, 1968-
  Veterinarian's tools / Mary Elizabeth Salzmann.
    p. cm. -- (Professional tools)
  ISBN 978-1-61613-582-9
  1. Veterinarians--Juvenile literature. 2. Veterinary medicine--Juve-
nile literature. 3. Veterinary instruments and apparatus--Juvenile
literature. I. Title.
  SF756.S25 2011
  636.089'0284--dc22
                        2010018601

Super SandCastle™ books are created by a team of professional
educators, reading specialists, and content developers around
five essential components—phonemic awareness, phonics,
vocabulary, text comprehension, and fluency—to assist young
readers as they develop reading skills and strategies and
increase their general knowledge. All books are written,
reviewed, and leveled for guided reading, early reading
intervention, and Accelerated Reader® programs for use in
shared, guided, and independent reading and writing activities to
support a balanced approach to literacy instruction.

CONTENTS

VISITING A VETERINARIAN

WHAT DOES A VETERINARIAN DO?

A veterinarian is an animal doctor. The vet's job is to help animals stay healthy. And if an animal gets sick, a vet can help it feel better.

WHY DO VETERINARIANS NEED TOOLS?

Tools help veterinarians to do their jobs better than they could without them. Special tools let veterinarians see, hear, and measure things in an animal's body.

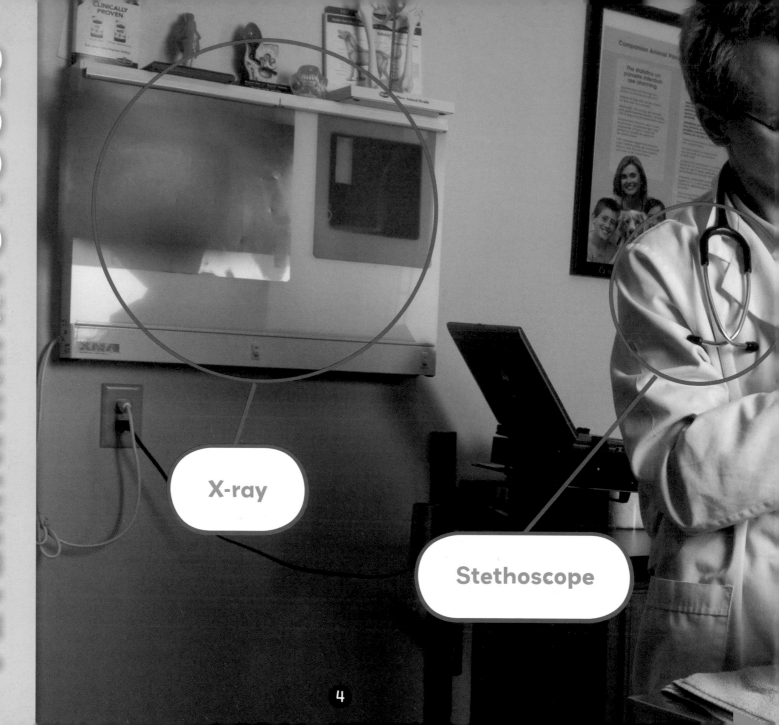

VETERINARIAN'S TOOLS

X-ray

Stethoscope

4

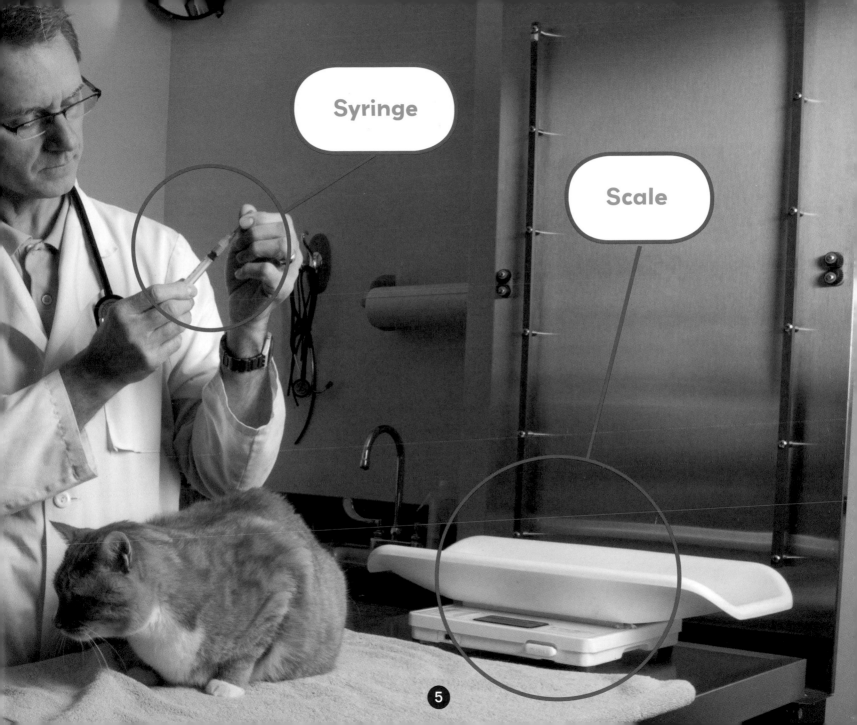

SCALE

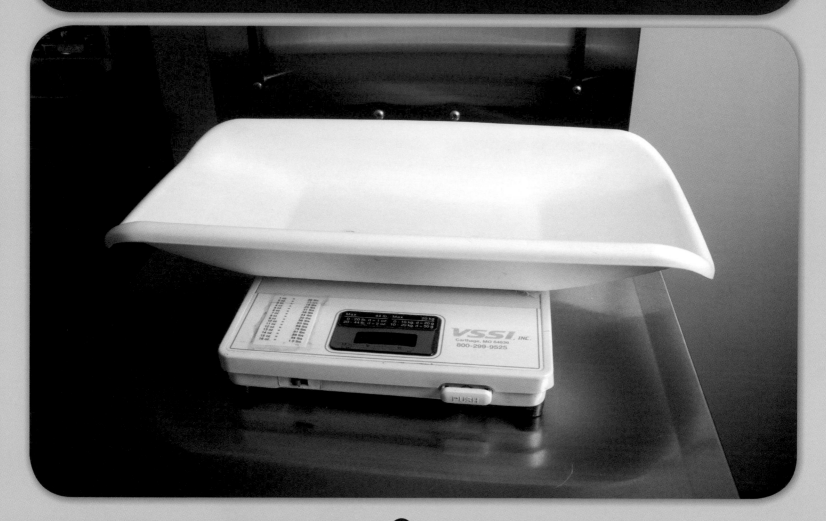

A scale is used to weigh animals.

A veterinarian uses a scale to see if an animal's weight is healthy.

If an animal is too fat, it could cause problems with its heart or **joints**.

If an animal has lost a lot of weight, that could mean it is sick.

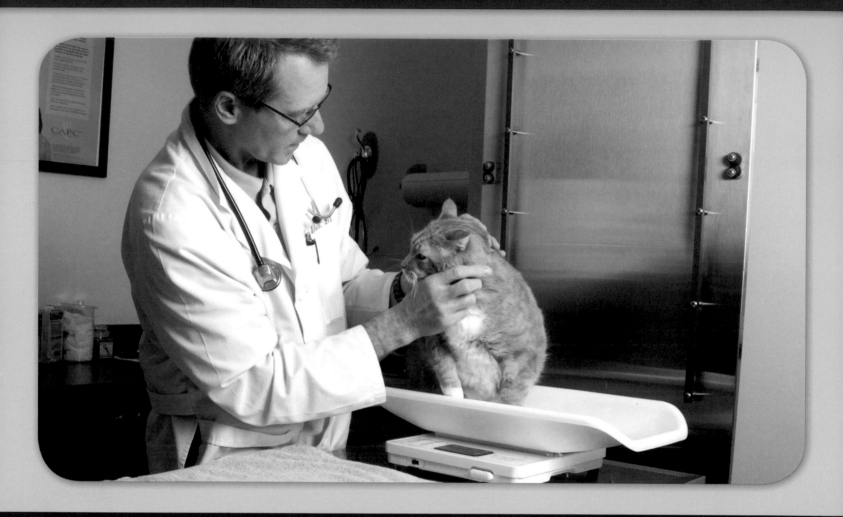

Dr. Ward weighs Cash on a table scale.
Cash weighs 15 pounds (7 kg).

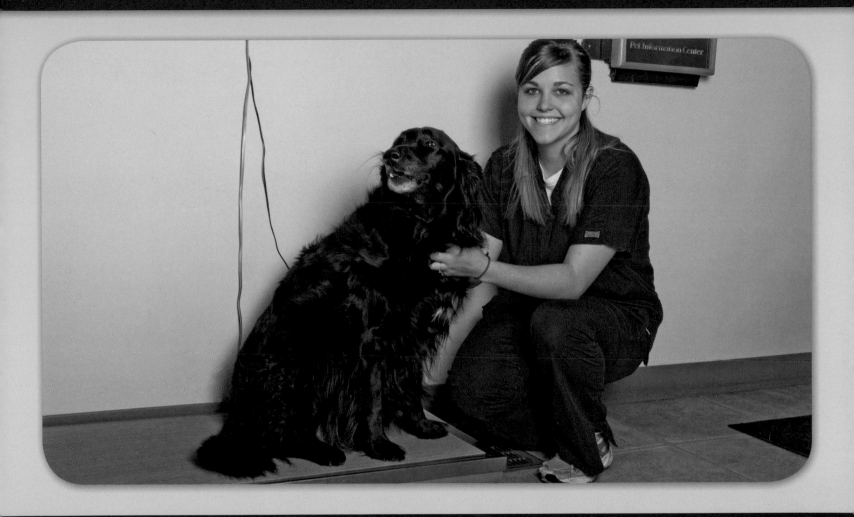

Wrigley is too big for a table scale. She gets weighed on a floor scale. Wrigley weighs 60 pounds (27 kg).

SYRINGE

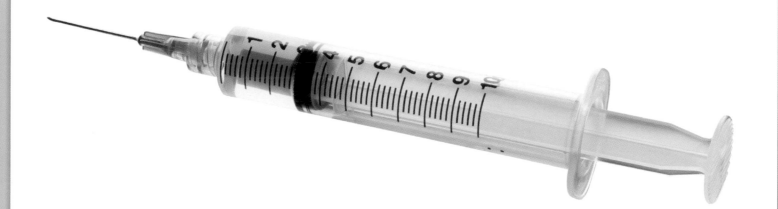

A syringe is used to give shots and take blood.

Veterinarians use syringes to give animals **medicine**. Some shots keep animals from getting sick. Other shots help sick animals get better.

Syringes can also be used to take small amounts of blood from animals. Vets test the blood to check for **diseases**.

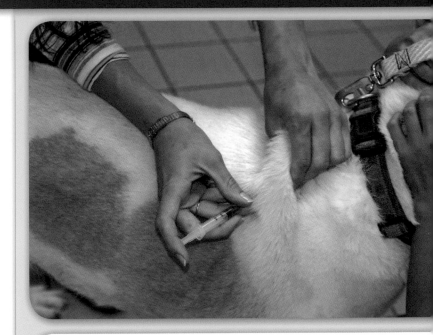

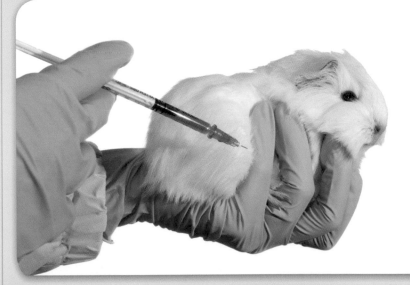

It's time for Buddy's checkup. Dr. Nestor gives him a shot so he won't get sick.

Maggie is sick. Dr. Upton uses a syringe to give her medicine to make her feel better.

X-RAY

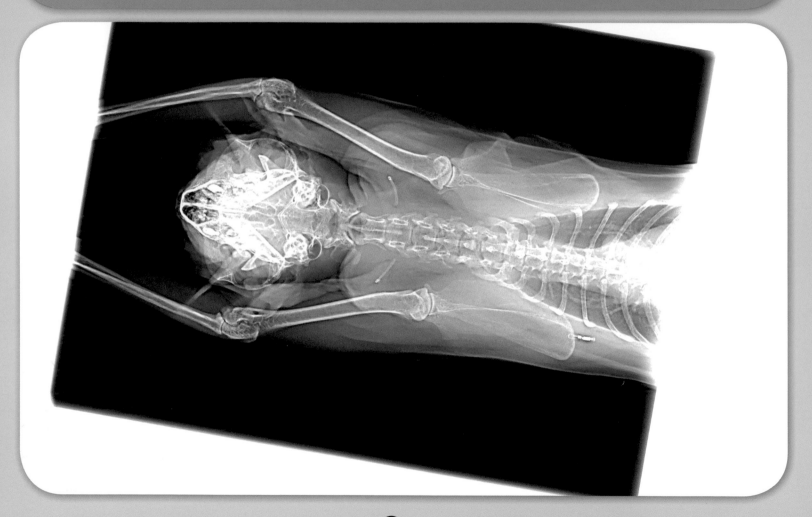

An X-ray is a picture of the inside of the body.

X-rays are made by an X-ray machine.

Bones show up best in an X-ray. A veterinarian uses an X-ray to see if a bone is broken.

X-rays can also be used to check the heart, **lungs**, and **muscles**.

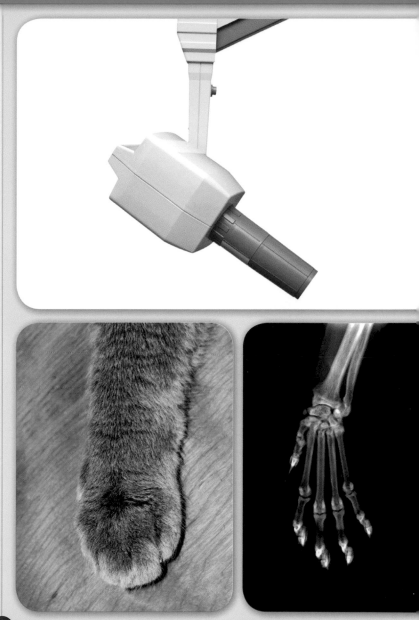

Lady is having an X-ray taken. Then the veterinarian will be able to see where she is hurt.

Dr. Grant is a veterinarian. He is looking at an X-ray of a dog's spine.

STETHOSCOPE

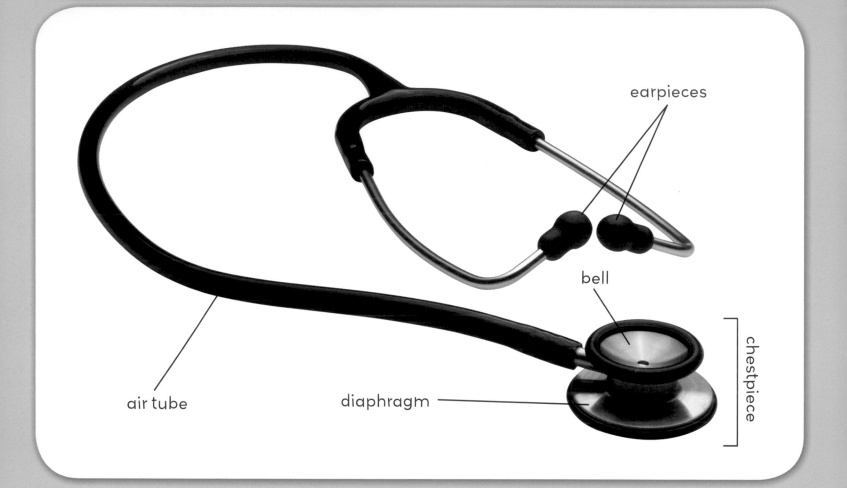

earpieces

bell

chestpiece

air tube

diaphragm

A stethoscope is used to listen to sounds inside an animal's body.

The veterinarian can listen to the animal's heart, **lungs**, or stomach. The vet places the chestpiece on the animal's body. Then the vet listens through the earpieces.

**Dr. Davis visits farms to take care of horses.
She uses a stethoscope to listen to a horse's heartbeat.**

Vicky and Isabel's dog Daisy is having a checkup.
Dr. Mills listens to Daisy's heart with a stethoscope.

MATCH THE WORDS TO THE PICTURES!

The answers are on the bottom of the page.

MATCH GAME

1. scale

a.

2. syringe

b.

3. X-ray

c.

4. stethoscope

d.

TEST YOUR TOOL KNOWLEDGE!

The answers are on the bottom of the page.

1.

A scale is used to weigh animals.

TRUE OR FALSE?

2.

Syringes are used to give animals shots.

TRUE OR FALSE?

3.

X-rays are pictures of the outside of an animal.

TRUE OR FALSE?

4.

A stethoscope is used to listen to an animal's heartbeat.

TRUE OR FALSE?

TOOL QUIZ

GLOSSARY

disease – a sickness.

film – a thin material you can see through that is used for taking pictures.

joint – a place on the body where bones meet, such as a knee or elbow.

lung – an organ in the body used for breathing air.

medicine – a drug used to cure or prevent disease.

muscle – the body tissue connected to the bones that allows people and animals to move.

pronounce – to say correctly.

spine – the row of small bones down the middle of a person or animal's back.